Alan Fowler has a career spanning the private and public sectors. He has held training and personnel appointments in the UK and overseas in four industries (engineering, shoe manufacture, sugar, construction) and two of the largest local authorities. He is currently Head of Manpower Services with Hampshire County Council, with a workforce of some 40,000.

He writes extensively on personnel topics, is a member of the Editorial Board of the IPM's journal (*Personnel Management*), a Fellow of the IPM, an employer member of the industrial tribunals, and Manpower Correspondent for the *Local Government Chronicle*. His two latest books are *Personnel Management in Local Government*, second edition published in 1980 by the IPM and *Local Authority Manpower* published in 1982 by BKT.

Getting off to a good start

Successful employee induction

Alan Fowler

INSTITUTE OF PERSONNEL MANAGEMENT

First published 1983
© *Institute of Personnel Management 1983*
All rights reserved

British Library Cataloguing in Publication Data

Fowler, Alan
    Getting off to a good start
    1. Employee induction—Great Britain
    I. Title
    658.3'1242'0941   HF 5549.5.153

ISBN   0 85292–332–5

Note: The convention has been followed whereby **he** and **him** are used to cover **she** and **her** wherever appropriate.

Printed in Great Britain by
Latimer Trend & Company Ltd, Plymouth

Contents

Introduction	1
1 THE EARLY LEAVER	3
Does early leaving matter?	5
Dealing with failures	6
The importance of induction	7
2 THE CAUSES OF EARLY LEAVING	8
False expectations during recruitment	8
Fitting into the organization	9
Fitting into the work group	10
Exit interviews	11
3 PRE-EMPLOYMENT ACTION	13
The job advertisement	13
The selection interview	14
Pre-employment documentation	16
company literature	16
conditions of employment	16
job descriptions	17
starting instructions	17
Conclusion	18
4 THE FIRST DAY AT WORK: RECEPTION AND DOCUMENTATION	20
Initial reception	20
Documentation	21

5 THE FIRST DAY AT WORK: INTRODUCTION
  TO THE WORKPLACE   23
  The supervisor   23
    the senior manager   24
  The starter's friend   25
  The job tutor   26
  Documents about the job   27
    job descriptions   27
    equipment manuals   27
    procedure schedules   28
  The trade union contact   29

6 THE INDUCTION COURSE: ATTENDANCE AND
  SCHEDULING   30
  Purpose of an induction course   30
  Choosing the course attenders   31
  Scheduling the course   32

7 THE INDUCTION COURSE: TECHNIQUES AND
  CONTENT   35
  Induction training techniques   35
    checklist of techniques   36
  Deciding the content   38
    checklist of content   39

8 COUNSELLING AND PROBATION   42
  Progress checks   43
    checklist of progress reviews   45
  The legal aspects of probation   47
  Probation documents   50
  Extending a probationary period   52

9 NEEDS OF PARTICULAR GROUPS   54
  School leavers   54

Graduates	56
Ethnic minorities	57
Industrial occupation groups	57
Managers	58
Transfers and promotions	60

10 THE ROLE OF THE PERSONNEL DEPARTMENT — 62
Designing policies and procedures — 62
   examples of induction policies — 63
Personnel department's own tasks — 64
Monitoring — 65
   statistics — 65
   other aspects — 66
Welfare and counselling — 67

Index — 69

Introduction

When organizations invest in new equipment they usually spend a good deal of time and money ensuring that it is properly installed, and that it is quickly brought up to the planned performance levels which justified its acquisition. Preventive maintenance systems are operated to avoid breakdowns. Detailed performance and cost records are kept of servicing, repairs and down-time.

This care and attention to new equipment is unhappily in stark contrast to the haphazard manner by which new employees are often inducted into their jobs. Inadequate training results in progress towards satisfactory work performance being slow and erratic. A failure to explain rules and regulations can lead to serious misunderstandings and to conflicts with colleagues or supervisors. Some new employees become disillusioned and resign; others may be dismissed for incompetence when an effective process of induction might well have resulted in success. Either way, avoidable direct and hidden costs arise. High rates of labour turnover push up recruitment costs. Low quality work, high error rates and unnecessarily lengthy learning periods raise unit costs.

The importance of operating effective induction systems cannot be over-emphasized. New employees need to have realistic expectations of their jobs. They need to be helped to fit rapidly into the organization and into the working group. They need to know clearly what is expected of them: the standards and style of the work they are to perform. They need to understand their organization's rules and regulations. They must know who's who at work, and who can make decisions about which issues. They should be helped to develop their aptitudes and talents. They need to feel that their employer has a respect for them as individuals, as potentially resourceful humans rather than as a mechanistic human resource.

This book is about effective induction and its purpose is to help all managers, whether in personnel or 'in the line', to achieve the highest possible success rate among new employees. Induction cannot be considered as a wholly separate function from other elements of personnel management. It has particular links with recruitment, selection and job training. It needs, too, to take account of some aspects of employment legislation. This book does not attempt to describe all these related matters in detail. Instead, it pulls together those elements of these other functions which have particular relevance to the management of new employees. It then sets these in a framework of induction procedures which span the period from job applicants' first contacts with their prospective employers until the time, many months after first starting work, when it is advisable to decide whether they have really made the grade.

Care and attention to induction will secure the same high levels of productivity and efficiency among new employees as planned installation and preventive maintenance can achieve for new machinery and equipment. The effort which is needed is undoubtedly worthwhile. The ultimate reward, apart from direct improvements in the organization's efficiency and competitiveness, is that the contribution which competent and highly motivated employees can make increases as years go by – unlike equipment, which begins to deteriorate from the first day it operates.

1
The early leaver

Employees are far more likely to resign during their first few months of employment than at any subsequent time. This phenomenon of 'the early leaver' has always been a problem for personnel managers, who see a high level of labour stability as one important characteristic of an effective, well-motivated labour force.

It is a persistent and very marked phenomenon. Writing of the period of full employment in the 1960s, Winifred Marks (the author of the IPM's first text on induction)[1], commented that in such a period: 'more people change jobs by choice than of necessity'. The inference was that early leaving was encouraged by full employment. Studies in the 1950s had shown that among factory workers, the proportion of leavers with less than three months service was quite commonly between 40 per cent and 50 per cent[2].

Yet moving into the 1980s, early leaving has not disappeared with the incidence of high levels of unemployment. Jobs may be hard to get and labour turnover may well have fallen overall. But of those employees who do leave, a large proportion is still those with very short service. One study in 1982 showed that some 30 per cent of female manual worker leavers had under three months service, and this from a relatively stable working group[3]. The same study indicated that there was a co-relation between the type of work and the pattern of early leaving. The table on page 4 illustrates this.

It can be seen that the figure for under three months service is highest for the least skilled group, and lowest for the highest skilled. Note, however, that the differences are less marked for the percentage of leavers with under 12 months service. It seems that the time taken by a new employee to size up the job, and to decide whether or not it is suitable or congenial is less for unskilled than for skilled workers, but that in the latter category a peak of leaving still occurs during a later but still early part of service.

Two other correlations may also exist. There seems to be a link between high levels of labour turnover and a high proportion of early

Category	% of leavers with	
	under 3 months service	under 12 months service
Manual workers (male & female): mainly unskilled & semi-skilled catering	23.3	32.4
White collar workers (female): mainly clerical staff, though including some specialists	13.1	31.8
White collar workers (male): mainly technical & professional staff	6.1	20.1

leavers. Very high turnover, for example 75 per cent on an annual basis, will usually be linked with very high proportions of leavers with very short service (about 50 per cent or more in the first three months). If general dissatisfaction with the work is widespread, then a higher proportion of employees than normal will decide to leave very soon after joining.

Secondly, there are indications that early leaving is reduced by an intensive initial training period. In the 1982 study referred to above, the figures for police and firemen were:

Category	% of leavers with	
	under 3 months service	under 12 months service
Firemen	3.6	7.1
Police	2.6	11.3

Both groups had very low levels of annual turnover (around 6 per cent), and a low proportion of early leavers is therefore to be expected. The percentages shown in the table, however, are very low indeed. It seems probable that this is connected with the fact that in both groups the new recruit has an intensive and full-time 12 week period of initial training followed by further on the job training, particularly during the first year of service. In both cases, too, selection procedures are more extensive and systematic than in much of industry, so the proportion of misfits should be considerably reduced. In these effects of selection and training there are lessons which form a major theme of this book. The use of statistics in monitoring early leavers is described in chapter 10 on page 65.

Does early leaving matter?

It may be asked, though, does a high proportion of short service leavers really matter? Is it, perhaps, merely a normal and largely unavoidable process of readjustment by which employees ultimately find the jobs which suit them?

There are at least three reasons for avoiding such complacency.

First, a high incidence of early leavers can be very expensive. Take, for example, a draughtsman on, say £6,500 pa. One leaves, giving a months notice, but it takes two months to recruit a replacement. The loss of output for the extra month (or overtime or agency payments to plug the gap) will cost at least £500, and recruitment costs (advertising, interview time, travelling expenses etc) may well add another £500. A replacement is recruited, but leaves after only two months. During these two months he has not been very effective and has taken up £500 worth of supervising time and that of some of his colleagues in abortive training and in the correction of mistakes. His own salary and on costs during this period have totalled around £1,500 and his actual output has not been worth more than, say, a third of this. Now the recruitment cycle has to be repeated. At a conservative estimate, therefore, the whole episode has had a net cost of around £2,500 and there is no guarantee that events will not be repeated next time around. If early leavers form one third of all leavers, and if the annual turnover rate is 25 per cent, then for a group of 100 such employees the annual costs of early leaving will total some £20,000 which is the equivalent of approximately three full-time staff. Cutting these costs, by reducing the incidence of premature departures, therefore appears to be a worthwhile management exercise.

There is a second reason for attempting such a reduction. Early leavers are often disillusioned and disgruntled. They tend to put all the blame on the employing organization with which they have patently failed to identify. Perhaps a few may have the insight and courage to say 'I made a mistake', but the majority will tell their family and friends that it was a rotten company. They will say that they were misled about pay or prospects, or that the management was abrasive or unsympathetic. In short, they will damage the organization's reputation as an employer. The more this occurs, the less easy it will be to find good quality recruits, and the likely result will be a repetition of early leaving.

Finally, one should not overlook the damage that a sequence of short stays can do to an employee's own career chances and aspirations. Personnel managers do, hopefully, have a concern for the well-being of individual employees, as well as for the interests of their companies. An employer with an early leaving problem is damaging not only his own efficiency: he is exacerbating the unemployment situation by contributing to the pool of job applicants whose employment histories damage their chances of getting interviews.

Dealing with failures

So far, we have commented only on the employees who resign. There are two other categories which should not be overlooked. First, there are those who are dismissed at a fairly early stage in their service. It is obviously wise to use the first few weeks or months of employment to weed out employees who fail to come up to standard, but who do not take the initiative themselves by resigning. If such dismissals are frequent, however, it must raise serious doubts about the adequacy of selection and initial training, and will certainly do harm to the employer's reputation.

Secondly, there is the other side to this particular coin: employees who should have been dismissed during the early or probation period, but due to lack of an effective appraisal system have been overlooked until some disaster befalls. Most personnel managers can quote cases of line managers seeking a dismissal on grounds of incapability a few days after the first 12 months of service have been completed, and so just outside the period during which a dismissed employee has no access to an industrial tribunal. Of course, dismissals are to be avoided if at all possible. Far better, through training and counselling, to rehabilitate. It would be idealistic, though, to claim that selection and training can be so infallible as to guarantee the total absence of the odd recruitment error and of the occasional 'wrong-un' among the new recruits. The effective use of the first few weeks or months of employment to check on suitability and capability, and to take whatever corrective action may be necessary (including dismissal) is an important aspect of the personnel management of the new employee. If a formal system of probationary service is used, the aspect of induction becomes even more significant. Formal confirmation of the satisfactory completion of probation sets a firmer seal on an employee's suitability than mere survival past the 12 month marker of unfair dismissal legislation. The principles, however, are the same.

The importance of induction

Induction, then, is about all the steps an employer can take to try to ensure that new recruits settle into their new jobs quickly, happily and effectively. It must include some aspects of pre-employment procedures, cover formal and informal training activities during the early part of an employee's service, consider the respective roles of line and personnel managers in the various procedures (particularly on counselling and on performance appraisal) and have regard to employment legislation when such issues as contracts of employment, formal probationary service and dismissals are dealt with.

In discussing the subject, too, one needs to distinguish the similarities and differences in induction needs of different categories of employees, and of different sectors of industry, commerce and public employment.

All the various aspects of the subject form the content of the subsequent chapters of this book. The underlying theme, which this first chapter has highlighted, is that a thorough, systematic and well-planned approach to induction carries dividends to the employer in helping to secure a competent, motivated workforce, and to the individual employee by contributing positively to career development.

References

1 *Induction – acclimatizing people to work* MARKS W R IPM 1970 (out of print)
2 *A Study of Labour Turnover,* EDC Committee for Food Manufacturing, 1967
3 Unpublished research by Hampshire County Council, 1982

2
The causes of early leaving

Before going into detail about various induction processes, it is useful to consider why employees often find the initial employment period a difficult one. There is no single explanation, and in any one case of employee failure (early resignation or dismissal) more than one factor may be involved. Consideration of the most common causes nevertheless helps to point the way for corrective or preventive action.

False expectations during recruitment

Perhaps the most elementary cause is when the job and conditions of service do not in practice match the expectations created during the recruitment process. A common and elementary mistake is for the recruiting manager to be over-optimistic about earnings. 'The basic rate's only £75 but there's a lot of overtime, and the bonus scheme can give you another third.' This sort of statement builds up an expectation of regular earnings of well over £100 per week. If, in practice, overtime is sporadic, and only employees with considerable experience maintain a one-third bonus, actual earnings for the newcomer may be little more than £80–£90 and disillusionment will soon set in.

Generalized and equally optimistic statements about promotion or training opportunities can also be damaging. An over-enthusiastic portrayal of 'prospects' may lure applicants into acceptances of job offers. They will not stay long if their workmates pour cold water on such statements, pointing to Tom, Dick and Harriet who have all been with the firm for years with no career progression whatsoever.

Similar misunderstandings may occur about the work itself. The recruiter may over-emphasize the unusual (and hence very interesting) but only occasional features of the job. Reality may show that in most weeks the work is simply boring routine. A related problem occurs when the newcomer finds great difficulty in determining just what the job is. A new customer service clerk may be told that work involves dealing with customer complaints and requests made by letter or telephone, but is given no checklist of typical problems or the correct procedures for dealing with them. A customer telephones with a complaint about a delayed delivery. The new clerk, using initiative, chases the factory production superintendent, only to be reproved for bypassing the proper channel of the production planning office. Such lack of clarity about who can make what decisions is a frequent source of frustration for the new employee in administrative, supervisory and managerial work. Inadequate or contradictory information as to how to obtain tools and materials and what to do if breakdowns occur, is similarly a worry to new manual workers. The whole situation is exacerbated if instructions appear to come from a variety of unpredictable sources. 'I just couldn't find out who expected me to do what!' or 'Nobody seemed to know what was happening', are typical comments made by early leavers who have experienced this kind of confusion.

A more direct problem arises if the new employee finds the work too difficult or if in the view of the management the new employee is incompetent. In the manual sector, the absence of aptitude tests for work requiring a high degree of dexterity or co-ordination may well result in selection failures becoming evident within the first few days. Inadequate numerative ability for an office job involving statistical manipulation may take longer to show itself. A lack of managerial capability in a very competent professional (engineer, accountant etc), promoted for the first time to a general managerial role, may not be evident for many months. It is in this type of situation that potential dismissals may feature as much as resignations. If required work standards are inadequately defined, the employee may not realize any shortfall. Resignations are likely only when the employee develops a strong sense of personal inadequacy and is reluctant to seek help.

Fitting into the organization

Another aspect of job difficulty arises when the new employee falls foul of supervision or management. The risk of a personality clash is greatest where the selection procedures do not involve the employee's immediate boss. Recruitment may have been handled entirely by the personnel department, or have involved only one line manager, and not the supervisor or foreman to whom the new employee is to report. On the new employee's first day at work when the foreman is met for the first time, they may take an instant dislike to each other, with inevitable consequences.

Less dramatically, the new employee may find the whole style of supervision and management uncongenial. Some organizations are highly participative, others are very authoritarian. One employee may find a high degree of definition and direction supportive; another (with previous experience, perhaps only of very informal organizations) will find the same situation repressive. Similarly, an absence of authoritative direction may worry some new employees, and generate feelings of uncertainty or inadequacy; while others will respond positively to a freedom to innovate or experiment. Few people are so rigid as to be wholly unable to adapt to different styles of management from those to which they have previously been accustomed. It is generally a matter of degree, combined with the extent to which management is aware of the problem and takes positive steps to aid the natural process of adaptation. 'I couldn't stand the manager!' nevertheless remains a very common explanation by an early leaver of the reasons for resignation.

Fitting into the work group

A less tangible cause of early leaving arises when the new employee has difficulty in adjusting to, or being assimilated into, the immediate working group. There is a mass of scientific evidence of the power and importance of group psychology.[1] The informal face-to-face working group develops its own style, standards and ethos quite separately from any formal organization structure or standards set by the company. Individuals within the group develop particular and different roles. There will be the unofficial leader, the joker, the conciliator, the innovator, the devil's advocate, and the kindly uncle. A well-established group will have a strong sense of its own identity with a tendency to treat outsiders with reserve, or possibly with good-natured scorn.

Into a cohesive group of this kind new employees are then injected, ie imposed from outside, not chosen by the group itself. What role are these newcomers to play? If they ignore the group's style and standards and work strictly to the formal, managerially defined system, the group will see them as a threat. They will therefore be frozen out or, at worst, actively obstructed.

Extreme situations of this kind are, however, less common than those in which the new employee merely feels a degree of incompatibility with the general attitude or style of the group.

For example the group's approach to work may be one of jovial cynicism about all company pronouncements about the need for higher productivity, which may conflict with the new employee's genuine desire to work hard and establish a good working reputation. Similarly, a group whose approach is to bend the rules to get results will make an uncongenial working environment for the over-particular administrator.

It may be very difficult to identify instances of incompatibility with groups. By their very nature, informal working groups lie outside the formal and known organizational systems and standards. Furthermore, employees who resign because of a generalized feeling that they are failing to fit in (a sense of being socially uncomfortable) are often reluctant or unable to explain this. They will give more obviously rational reasons for leaving: 'I don't like the work': 'I can get more money somewhere else', rather than delve into the very much more diffuse and complex reasons for their unhappiness at work.

Exit interviews

Identifying the real reasons for the failure of new employees to perform or fit in, is thus not as simple as may first appear. The reason given by the employee may not be the basic reason: there may be a multiplicity of influences on the final decision to leave. Knowing what these reasons are nevertheless lies at the basis of all corrective action. The design of an effective induction process may thus well start with an analysis of leavers' attitudes and problems, obtained by the personnel manager interviewing all employees who resign. Termination interviews can be time-consuming and demand considerable skill if they are to reveal the underlying reasons for an unsatisfactory level of labour turnover. They may even be considered undesirable by some supervisors who see them as a threat; i.e. the personnel manager listening to ill-founded complaints by malcontents! But no personnel manager who wishes to ensure that the induction process fully matches the needs of the organization can afford to disregard this very direct source of information about what causes employees to resign (see also pages 66 and 67).

Reference

1 There is a great deal of literature about working groups going back at least to the famous Hawthorne studies of Elton Mayo in 1924–32 (See *Management and the*

Worker, ROETHLISBERGER F J, *and* DICKSON W J, Harvard University Press, 1939, and *Organizational Psychology,* SCHEIN E H, Prentice Hall, 1970)

A useful summary of this, and other studies is given in chapter 2 of *Elements of Personnel Management,* PRATT K J *and* BENNETT S G, Gee & Co Ltd, 1979.

3
Pre-employment action

All new employees start work with some expectations about their new jobs. These ideas are gained during the recruitment process and their accuracy or inaccuracy can have a significant impact on labour turnover during the critical first few weeks of employment. Disillusionment, if reality proves less attractive than an over-rosy picture painted during recruitment, is a potent cause of early leaving. More positively, some preparation for assimilation into the new job can be achieved before the first day at work, and so expedite the later induction process.

The job advertisement

Impressions about an employer begin to form even on first reading a job advertisement. Is the style formal or informal? What is given most emphasis: job content or job benefits? Even the visual impact of the advertisement has an influence. Is it drab and old-fashioned in layout and type-face, or does it come across as modern, attractive, imaginative? From an induction viewpoint, this image and reality should be reasonably coincident.

Consider one extreme type of job advertisement; those which suggest very high rewards but say little or nothing about the actual work. 'Do you want to earn £500 per week?' These are almost always for direct selling jobs, on a self-employed basis or on a low basic wage plus high commission. Labour turnover during the first few weeks in such work is so high that advertising has to be all but continuous. Perhaps the companies concerned would do better if their advertisements stressed the independence of the self-employed worker and the need in this kind of work for dogged persistence, rather than dangling a lure of apparently easy money. Over-optimism in job advertisements about earnings is a recipe for serious disappointment and reaction from new recruits.

Disillusionment can also occur through differences in style or character between the job advertisement and the working environment. An over-imaginative advertising agency, or an enthusiastic but inexperienced personnel manager, may persuade a company to jazz up its advertisements with bright and breezy images and phraseology. The advertisement for customer service clerks, for example, may carry a photograph of a young, smart, smiling office worker, slimline telephone tucked under the chin, sitting at a glass and steel desk, backed by impressive office foliage. Suppose, however, that reality is a very ordinary office with the usual motley collection of wooden furniture, standard black telephones, and a mainly middle-aged workforce. There may well be a case for refurbishing the office, but it needs to be done before the recruitment campaign begins, not after several young recruits have resigned.

It is to be hoped, too, that those employers (generally in the public sector) who emblazon all their advertisements with the proud claim 'We are an Equal Opportunity Employer' really live up to their word. To eradicate prejudice and covert discrimination throughout a large organization requires very much more effort than inserting a slogan in staff advertisements.

The selection interview

What occurs during selection interviews is of even more importance than the job advertisement. Here, for the first time, the potential new employee makes a personal contact with the potential employer, and may see the actual workplace and meet his or her potential manager or supervisor. The opportunity arises (or should do) for the applicant to ask questions, as well as to be told about the organization and the job.

In practice, the extremes of approach are very wide.

In one case, only one interview may be conducted by a recruitment officer (not the potential supervisor) at a hotel, or in the offices of the local jobcentre. Because of time pressures the interview may be very one-sided, with no opportunity for the applicant to ask questions. Little or no recruitment literature may be provided. Job offers may be made by letter and include little more than basic information about conditions of employment. With this type of recruitment procedure, new employees on their first day at work will be almost as ignorant of what the job and the employing organization are really like as when they first saw the job advertisement.

At the other extreme, candidates may be assembled in a group before the interviews start, and given a talk about the organization, possibly supplemented with a film. They will meet on the working premises and in addition to the personnel manager will meet line managers and their own potential direct supervisors. Before or after the interviews there will be a conducted visit around the establishment and the whole process may end with a session in which the candidates can ask questions of a panel of the selecting staff. When a procedure of this kind has been followed, a start has been made to a formal induction programme before the new employee actually starts work. Not only will all the key information have been provided about the job and conditions of employment, but by meeting their potential bosses and by seeing the work location, new employees should have gained a good general impression of what working at this particular organization would be like. The only danger arises when this type of highly structured pre-induction becomes much better organized than the work processes themselves. If potential employees are looked after better during selection than when at work, some disappointment is inevitable.

A less formal, but still thorough approach may be better suited to most circumstances. A typical programme for an individual applicant may be along these lines:

10.00 am: Initial interview with personnel manager

10.45 am: If applicant considered a 'possible' conducted to workshop or office to meet potential supervisor. Supervisor walks applicant round to show work location and type of work in progress, followed by interview in supervisor's office

11.45 am: Applicant returned to personnel officer, either for immediate offer to be made, or to be told when and how outcome of interview to be notified. This session also used for applicant to ask questions, and to be told more about conditions of employment.

Essential elements of this routine are the quick, informal walk-through of the workplace; and the opportunity for applicant and supervisor to size each other up. The first day at work will not carry the terrors of the unknown if this important ice-breaking has been achieved earlier and before the applicant is irrevocably committed to employment.

Pre-employment documentation

There are four types of document which should be considered in the pre-employment period: literature about the organization, details of conditions of employment, job descriptions and instructions about the first day at work.

Company literature

This type of information provides some general scene-setting about company organization, size and functions; and begins to foster an interest and pride in being its employee. Some thought needs to be given in order to match the type of literature to the kind of employees to whom it is issued. New managerial staff will not take kindly to being given a too obviously idiots' guide: while 16 year old school leavers starting in unskilled jobs are unlikely to be enthused by a copy of last year's annual report and accounts.

For pre-induction purposes, all such literature has a somewhat limited value. New employees' over-riding concern is with the details of their new jobs: an interest in the wider company scene develops on the foundation of integration within the particular workplace.

Conditions of employment

These documents are of great importance, not only legally, but because the information they contain about earnings, pensions, holidays, hours of work and so on plays an important part in the applicant's decision to accept an offer of employment. To avoid later problems, and ensure that the potential employee has a thorough and accurate understanding of the terms of service, these documents need to be comprehensive, but also easy to understand.

The formal contract of employment, or the standard schedule of terms and conditions, may have to be written in a fairly terse and legalistic style. For a number of important items no more may be said than, for example: 'Overtime is paid in accordance with the National Agreement for the industry's manual workers'. The formal information about pensions (a critically important employee benefit for many applicants) may use unexplained jargon such as 'reckonable service may exceed pensionable service but counts only towards qualifying periods'. An explanatory leaflet or booklet about all the important conditions of service, including pensions, written in an informal, easy-to-read style is of great assistance in ensuring that new employees do understand their entitlements. It should certainly include details of items, covered by national agreements, which are not set out in the formal documents. To protect the employer's legal position, the explanatory leaflet may need to include a statement to the effect that 'The purpose of this leaflet is solely to help employees understand the details of the company's conditions of employment and does not form part of the contract of employment.'

Job descriptions
Job descriptions may also be issued with the formal contract documents. It is advisable for them not to form part of the actual contract as this may inhibit flexibility in deployment at a later stage, but as a guide to the nature of the work they are extremely useful. Any apparent differences between the formal contract and the job description should be explained. For example, the contract may specify only a very general form of appointment such as 'assistant administrator', and state that the employee may be required to work 'in such departments and locations as the company may from time to time require'. The job description, however, may be very specific and set out the duties for a particular post, say, 'sales office administrative assistant'. This is the job in which the new employee is to start, but from which a transfer may be made at any time. To avoid later misunderstandings, it is essential that the new employee understands the difference between the first appointment and the wider contractual obligation to accept transfers to other work. Ambiguities must be eliminated from all pre-employment documentation.

Chapter 5, page 27 deals with job descriptions as working documents once employment has begun.

Starting instructions
Instructions given or sent to the new employee before employment starts bring the new employee to the door on his or her first day. They should be helpfully explicit about such basic details as where and when to report on the first day and what, if anything, to bring. A checklist shows the number of points about which the new employee may worry if no information is provided:

Time: should this be the standard starting time, or a little later to ensure that reception staff, supervisors, etc, are present when the new employee arrives?

Place: which entrance should be used? If reporting to a department, which location or room number?

Person to see: who is first going to see the new employee, or for whom should he or she ask?

Car parking: if the new employee is likely to travel to work by car, where should the car be parked?

Clothing: are there rules about clothing at work? Or will protective clothing be issued?

Tools: is the employee expected to supply his own tool kit?

Documents: is a reminder necessary about bringing documents such as the P45, and a signed copy of the contract of employment?

Security: are any instructions necessary about security? Is it necessary to show the starting letter or a pass to the security staff?

Catering: would a brief reminder about the company's catering facilities be helpful?

Medical examination: does the new employee have to undergo a medical examination?

New employees are often worried that on arrival on their first day they may use the wrong entrance, or lose their way in complex office or factory premises. In a large organization, a sketch map, showing the right entrance and the reporting location, is of great help. They also want to know who they are going to meet, who should be preferably someone they have already met during the recruitment process. For some types of work they may worry, too, about wearing the right clothes; a point that may be touched on during recruitment, but which should be repeated in the starting instruction if the matter is at all important.

Conclusion

Pre-employment induction will have served its purpose if the new employee can look forward to the first day at work with some confidence. On going home at the end of the day, the new employee's family will ask: 'What was it like?' If pre-employment induction has been effective, the answer should be along the lines, 'Not bad, and very much what I expected.'

References

For comprehensive coverage of all aspects of recruitment and selection, see:
Recruitment and Selection, PLUMBLEY P R, IPM, 1976
Contracts at Work, SUTER E, IPM, 1982

4
The first day at work: reception and documentation

However well-prepared the new starter may be, some trepidation about the first day in a new job will always remain. Although this may be more marked for the school leaver who is entering paid employment for the first time, even senior managers starting in a new appointment will, if they are honest, admit to first day nerves. The importance of planned induction on the first day is therefore obvious, although there is also a risk of attempting too much in one day. A too-intensive one-day programme of introductions to numerous members of staff, tours of the factory or office, and a series of talks about the organization and about conditions of employment, could well be more confusing and stressful than merely starting the actual job with little preparation.

It must be remembered that new employees on their first day will not be wholly relaxed, and will be primarily concerned with immediate practical matters such as locating their workplace, the lavatories and the canteen. They will not be receptive to a great mass of new information, particularly if much of it has no immediate relevance to the over-riding need to get through the first day without making some embarrassing mistake.

Initial reception

As noted on page 17, the letter confirming the appointment should ensure that the new employee gets to the right reception point at the right time. If all new starters have to report to a general reception desk, the receptionist should be provided with a list of those expected each day, with instructions about where they are to be directed. An informal welcoming word from the receptionist, showing that the employee is expected and making an initial human contact, will get the day off to a good start.

The importance of this first contact can be emphasized by looking at the effect of a badly organized introduction. Here, the new starter goes to a reception point, only to find it unmanned. After a worrying wait, a receptionist appears, takes the newcomer's name and, after looking puzzled, asks the starter to wait. The receptionist, possibly a general purpose security officer, then picks up the telephone and can be heard to say: 'I've got a Miss Jones here who says she's starting work in Accounts. What do you want me to do with her?' After some further telephone chat, the receptionist says to Miss Jones: 'You're in the wrong place; you should have gone to the staff entrance to the Adminblock – it's down the stairs, turn right, across the yard, left by Goods Inwards, and through the green doors in the old building nearly opposite behind the car park.' Miss Jones will eventually arrive at her workplace late, flustered, in no state of mind to absorb detailed instructions about her job, and with a first impression of being a very small and not well-meshed cog in an impersonal and unfriendly organizational machine.

Not all organizations require starters to report to a general reception point. In some offices or factories, new employees go direct to their section manager's office. In large-scale retailing, they will most likely report to the staff manager. In construction, the site labour officer or the general foreman may be their first contact. In many organizations, all new starters report on their first morning to the personnel office. Whatever the precise arrangements, the same checklist can be applied:

(i) ensure that the person who the starters first meet, ie the receptionist, secretary, personnel assistant, knows of their pending arrival and what to do next
(ii) set a reporting time which will avoid the risk of the starter turning up before the reception or office staff arrive
(iii) train reception staff in the need for friendly and efficient helpfulness towards new starters
(iv) if the new starter has to go on to another location immediately after reporting, provide a guide unless the route to the other location is very straightforward
(v) avoid keeping the new starter waiting: steady, unhurried, guided activity is an excellent antidote to first day nerves.

Documentation

Once past the initial reception point, one of the first formalities is to complete any necessary employment documentation. The new starter will be requested to hand over the P45 income tax form from the previous employer, or in its absence may need an explanation of the resultant emergency tax coding. There may also be a card or form of some kind to complete from an employment agency. The organization itself may issue a variety of documents to new employees, some of which may require signatures for their receipt. These may include:

    employee handbook
    identity card or security pass
    canteen pass or tokens
    clock card or time clock key
    locker keys
    car park permit
    authorization to draw protective clothing or tools from stores
    membership card for social club
    documentation for company car
    company rule book: including details of disciplinary and grievance procedures
    safety rules and safety literature.

It may also be necessary for the employee to provide some information for personnel records, additional to that obtained during the selection process. This might include:

    details of next of kin, with telephone contact during working hours
    name and address of GP, if required for medical check
    details of own car, if this is to be used for work
    driving licence and car insurance certificate
      (certificate may require endorsement for business use)
    first aid certificate, if relevant
    birth certificate – for pension or life insurance records
    passport or work permit, if not a UK citizen
    trade union membership details, if needed for union membership agreements.

These checklists illustrate one possible danger, that of overburdening the starter with too much initial information, and with too many documents. If some of the items listed are not essential on the first day, there is much to be said for issuing only the most necessary then, and dealing with the others over the next few days.

5
The first day at work: introduction to the workplace

Unless starters spend their first day attending some form of training course (a procedure discussed in the next chapter) the first day will require a planned introduction to the actual workplace.

Starters will have three immediate concerns about the actual workplace.

(i)   What is the geography? What routes should be taken to and from the main entrance? Where are the time clocks (if any)? Where are the lavatories? Where is the canteen?
(ii) Who's who? Who and where is the immediate supervisor, the section manager, other important staff? Who are the immediate working colleagues? Who allocates the work? Who is going to explain what?
(iii) What work is actually going to be done during the first day?

For induction purposes, the most important question here is: who is going to explain what? The answer is most unlikely to be a single person. No supervisor is likely to have sufficient time to explain all the many practical details involved, though all supervisors should accept a heavy personal involvement in the induction of newcomers. A useful approach may therefore involve three people: the supervisor, a 'starter's friend' and a job tutor.

The supervisor

It is essential that the new employee is met at the workplace by his or her supervisor. The same supervisor will preferably have taken part in the final selection process, so that this should not be a meeting of strangers. If this is not possible, the person to receive and welcome the newcomer to the department or section should be the supervisor or manager to whom the new employee will report on a day to day basis.

The quality of the personal relationship between supervisors and their employees is extremely important, and this first meeting can set the tone for the future. It is the supervisor's first opportunity to establish a positive rapport with his employees, and a friendly, helpful but firm and positive approach to this first meeting will do much to establish the supervisor's later influence. The induction of new employees should form part of any supervisor's training, and it is a responsibility that supervisors must be encouraged and expected to take seriously.

The supervisor, then, should be the first to meet the new employee, and explain some of the initial do's and dont's. Some aspects of induction may be delegated to other staff, but information about timekeeping and any important safety regulations should come directly from the supervisor. Only by such direct explanation will the importance of the principal rules and regulations affecting everyday working life be sufficiently emphasized.

In some sectors, other essential points may require similar personal emphasis by the supervisor, such as:

(i)   In manufacturing, the key rules about quality standards, the reporting of breakages or tool losses.
(ii) In retailing, rules about staff purchases, customer complaints and stores security.
(iii) In offices, any standard drills for answering external telephone calls, or for the style of official letters.
(iv) In some local government jobs, key points about staff conduct relative to elected members, the public and the press.

The senior manager
Either on the first day, or as soon as possible thereafter, the supervisor should introduce the new starter to the appropriate senior manager who has overall responsibility for the department or location. The size and type of the organization will determine who this should be. Obviously, in a large multi-plant company the managing director cannot meet every new shopfloor or office worker. But senior managers should make every effort to meet as many of their employees as possible.

It is a particular feature of Japanese management, including Japanese plants in the UK, that the factory manager meets each new starter and so establishes a personal contact at the earliest stage of employment. UK managers are often criticized by their workforce for being too remote. A routine in which the supervisors introduce their new workers to their senior managers can go some way to establishing better working relationships. The investment of a little managerial time in showing an interest in employees as individuals will be amply repaid by the positive and co-operative attitudes it can help to promote.

The starter's friend

The supervisor should also introduce the new employee to his or her immediate work group and to the group's leading hand or section senior.

One of this group should be selected to act as the starter's initial guide, primarily to ensure a knowledge of the geography and perhaps to provide practical tips about the more informal do's and dont's of working life. It is helpful for this 'starter's friend' to be the same sex and of similar age and background to the new employee. A middle-aged woman is unlikely to feel at home being shown round by a teenage lad, or *vice versa*, particularly as washrooms and lavatories need to be included in the itinerary.

There is also much to be said for these initial guides to have fairly short service. As relative newcomers, they are likely to remember all the little points which were a potential source of worry to them when they started work, and so help new starters learn the ropes rapidly.

They should, of course, be selected for this work in advance of starters arriving, and given some basic instruction as to what is needed. It is helpful to issue them with a short checklist of points to be covered in the first day. It is likely to include the following:

- location of entrances and exits and time clocks
- routes to and from the canteen, lavatories, car park, rest room, first-aid room, supervisor's/manager's/personnel department's offices
- location and any particular procedures for cloakrooms, changing rooms, tool or clothing stores
- location of vending machines and purchasing system (eg tokens)
- canteen procedures (eg cash, tokens, authorization cards etc). Tips about informal canteen customs, ie who usually sits where and when, will also prevent unnecessary embarrassment.

The type of employee needed as a starter's friend is one who will be helpful but not overbearing, good at explanation, sufficiently relaxed to be relied on to chat about informal aspects of the job, and reliable in the sense of covering the necessary ground and not passing on bad working customs. It is also cost effective to use a more junior employee in this role rather than to take up the time of higher paid supervisory staff.

The job tutor

The right person to act as guide may not be the right employee to teach the new employee the actual work involved in the job. For this, an experienced employee is essential and one who has been trained in the skills of job instruction. It is not unusual for this task to be allocated to the leading hand or section head of the working unit. Where this is not so, it is still a function which needs to be recognized as of critical importance, and for which preparation is essential. Even if supervisors have insufficient time to train new starters personally, it is essential that they monitor the quality of the job training carried out in their sections. However busy they are with other duties, they should certainly take time to check the progress of every new starter at frequent intervals and to reinforce key elements of job training by personal instruction.

The full process of learning the new job may, of course, take many weeks. In much work it is aided by some form of off the job instruction. For some activities an initial full-time training period in a training section or a separate training centre may be essential (see chapters 6 and 7). Here, we are considering only the first working day for jobs where the new starter is not required to follow a formal job training programme.

There are, perhaps, two complementary principles for the trainer (supervisor or experienced worker) to bear in mind for this first day:

(i) Do not overload the new employee with too much information. For the first day, the simple basics of the job are adequate. Have a training programme which takes in the wider or more complex elements of the job on a phased basis over subsequent days.
(ii) Do keep the new employee busy. There is little worse for an ill-at-ease newcomer than having nothing to do. The new employee can be made to feel embarrassingly isolated and conspicuous if left sitting at an empty desk, or standing at an idle machine, while everything around is a hive of activity.

The emphasis should be on an explanation and demonstration of a few of the basic work tasks, and the allocation of sufficient appropriate work to enable the starter to do something useful without too much obvious supervision. Trying to cope with a new job under direct and continuous observation is particularly trying. What is needed is a fairly frequent check on progress, without breathing down the newcomer's neck.

Documents about the job

Three types of document may assist the initial job learning process: job descriptions, equipment manuals, and job or procedure schedules.

Job descriptions
These may have been included in the documentation issued before starting work. At this stage they may have seemed rather formal or abstract. On the first day they gain significance and should be used by the supervisor or section head as an aid to job instruction. They may, for example, be used as a check-list, showing the starter which elements of the whole job have been covered in the first day, and which have been deferred until later in the learning process. It is often important to emphasize to new starters that the job description is a general guide and not a wholly comprehensive or restrictive schedule, and also that other duties generally appropriate to the job may occur from time to time. As noted in chapter 3, page 17, there may also be a need to explain the possibility of transfers to other work not covered in the description of the initial job.

Equipment manuals
These should always be available for typewriters, word processors, photocopiers and other similar equipment. It is usually necessary to demonstrate the operation of such machines to new starters who are unfamiliar with the particular models in use, but instruction manuals should also be issued. Many typists, for example, prefer to learn the operation of new typewriter models by teaching themselves from the equipment manual, rather than by having to rely on their supervisor's or colleagues' tuition. Some manufacturers' manuals, however, are very poorly written for teaching purposes, and may need supplementing or replacing by a clearer set of operating instructions written by the organization's own training staff. Office staff should also be provided with their company's general *sales literature*. This will help to ensure that they project the image of a well-informed workforce and will develop their interest in the ideals and objectives of the organization for which they work.

Procedure schedules
Schedules of working procedures should be used more widely. Too often, new employees have to learn for themselves how particular elements of the work ought to be done, or what procedures to follow to undertake particular job functions. Job descriptions tend to emphasize responsibilities, eg 'responsible for daily sorting and distribution of internal mail', but do not say how these responsibilities are actually discharged. A simple schedule for the mail job shows how much more helpful to the newcomer is a procedure manual:

Daily procedure for internal mail
1 Between 9.00 am and 9.30 am each morning, collect mail from pigeon hole E in room 218.
2 Open all mail, except sealed envelopes marked 'personal' and/or 'confidential'.
3 Stamp all opened mail and all unopened private/confidential envelopes with date and time stamp.
4 Sort mail into six trays (marked with section titles), using internal phone directory to identify relevant sections where only employees' names are given.
5 Refer any queries to administrative manager in room 103.
6 Take sorted mail to the six section heads (room numbers shown on trays): should be completed by 10.15 am
    etc   etc   etc.

Obviously, different procedure schedules will apply to different types of work, but the principle of setting out a step-by-step instruction for all the main working tasks can be applied to almost all jobs. For a simple factory task, for example, a schedule might be along these lines:

Packing procedure
1 Take packing box from pallet at left of machine and place on left side of packing bench.
2 Take two polystyrene packing pieces from bin A and fit over ends of completed unit.
3 Place packed unit into box, top side up.
4 Lay instruction leaflet and guarantee card on top of unit.
5 Seal box with tape from dispenser on right of bench, as shown in diagram on wall.
6 Place sealed box on pallet at right of bench.

At more senior levels, the documentation of procedures for such matters as obtaining staff, placing purchasing orders, reporting production or other results, reporting accidents or stock losses, aids the rapid adaptation of new staff, and eases the burden of training or explanation by existing supervisors and managers.

The trade union contact

Apart from the section supervisor and working colleagues, there may be one other personal introduction to be made on this first day: to the section or departmental shop steward. This will depend on the procedures agreed with the trade unions and in some organizations may not apply at all. In others, unions may be supplied with names and work locations of new starters and any personal follow-up is left to the shop stewards. Where employees are highly unionized (whether by custom and practice, or by a closed shop agreement) a personal introduction by the section supervisor may, however, be desirable. Even if this is not considered necessary, new employees should certainly be told if they are likely to be approached by the stewards; and given an indication of the organization's attitude to union membership. The form of these explanations might be:

> A Mr Brown may come and see you. He's the shop steward for the T & GWU. It is entirely up to you whether you join or not. There is no closed shop and the company considers that it is something about which employees should make up their own minds without any pressure either way.

Or:

> Mr Brown, our T & GWU shop steward will be seeing you soon. We don't run a closed shop, but by and large we think it is a good thing for most people to join unless they have very strong views against.

It is as well, too, to have an understanding with the trade unions about the nature of their approach to new employees, particularly if several unions are competing for membership. It is undesirable in such situations for one particular steward, who happens to get in first, to give a new employee the impression that only that union exists, if within a short period the employee is going to be approached by one or two other recognized unions.

6
The induction course: attendance and scheduling

Many employers, particularly those with large numbers of employees and consequently significant numbers of recruits, find it helpful to deal with induction on a more formal basis than has been discussed in the last two chapters. In short, to run induction courses.

Purpose of an induction course

There are several reasons for this:

> dealing with recruits in groups saves considerable time which would otherwise be spent by personnel managers and supervisors going over the same ground with each individual starter

> an efficiently planned training course will ensure that all necessary information is relayed consistently to all new starters. It will guard against the omissions which can so easily arise if induction is left to *ad hoc* action by busy supervisors

> within an effectively designed induction course, a full range of techniques can be used to assist in the assimilation of information: films and other visual aids, discussions, 'chalk and talk' lectures, planned visits, working projects. Few of these techniques can be used during informal induction.

At the same time, there are some potential dangers in relying wholly or mainly on formally organized courses. In particular:

> an induction course may be far more organized than 'real life'. It may be highly structured not only in its content but in terms of its hour to hour organization. Trainees may, in effect, be so spoon-fed on the course that the eventual transfer to work may constitute the very kind of culture shock which induction is designed to prevent

> trainees may suffer from a surfeit of information if all induction is packed into one training course at the beginning of employment.

Any induction course has to include a fair volume of information, much of it detailed. Furthermore, some of this information is likely to be fairly remote from day to day working experience. For example, an explanation of company structure, or of a complex pension scheme, has little immediate relevance to a young starter in a fairly basic job

if only personnel and training staff are involved in running induction courses, starters are left unassisted on one most important element in their induction: their absorption into the social fabric of the organization. Getting to know line managers and supervisors and adjusting to their style; 'tuning in' to the ethos and attitudes of working groups; these are aspects of induction which cannot be dealt with by personnel and training staff alone within the confines of a formal training course.

Despite these potential risks, any organization which has a sufficient inflow of new recruits to provide satisfactory training groups is likely to find that the benefits of an induction course far outweigh any disadvantages.

In planning such a course, a number of factors need to be considered:

should the course be designed for a single category of staff, or draw together new starters from a variety of occupations and levels?

how should it be structured and scheduled? Possibilities include a single half or whole day on the first day at work: a much longer initial period in which induction training merges into initial job training (perhaps in a training centre): a course covering several days but spread over a number of weeks on a day-release basis

what training techniques are to be used? (films, talks, discussions, visits, etc)

how much of the whole process of induction should be included in the course, and how much left for managers and supervisors to deal with at the workplace?

Choosing the course attenders

If the organization employs large numbers of staff within one particular category (eg retail shop assistants in a large departmental store: semi-skilled, general purpose factory workers in a large assembly plant) the induction course can be designed specifically for this group. It can concentrate on the very specific details of one particular type of work, and may then be linked very readily with initial job training.

But many organizations are multi-functional and even the simpler type of company will have a sprinkling of new starters in other types of work than the main occupation. If an induction course is then limited to matters which affect all employees, rather than dealing with the specifics of one occupation, it is possible to bring together, for induction purposes, starters for a variety of jobs. The new craftsman, the new clerk, the new storekeeper, all share some common information needs about the organization, its function and its employment rules and regulations and can all attend the same training programme for these particular induction elements. Mixing occupations together in this way may help, too, in creating cohesive and co-operative attitudes between different sectors of the workforce.

On this basis, all the new starters on a particular day, whatever their jobs, will be kept together for at least the initial part of the induction programme.

Some organizations mix, not only different occupations, but widely different levels of staff; though this is, perhaps, a more debatable practice. It must depend on the style of the organization. If the emphasis is very much on reducing status differences, then it is appropriate for the new manager or supervisor to attend the same induction course as the new clerk or factory worker. If the view is that the authority and standing of senior staff should be reinforced, then separate induction is indicated. The actual content of an induction programme may also influence this point. For example, mixing a large number of staff from various levels for a film about company operations overseas may be entirely satisfactory, while to do the same thing for a session explaining and discussing disciplinary and grievance procedures would be inappropriate.

In the large organization a variety of approaches can be developed. All new employees may come together for some very general background about the company as a whole. Multi-occupational groups may share sessions on common employment practices, while smaller groups may be more appropriate for more detailed induction, specific to particular types of work.

Scheduling the course

The timing and length of an induction course will be influenced by decisions about who attends and about its content. There are, though, some general points which should be considered and which influence the final design of the course.

The danger of attempting too much too soon applies to all types of employees and organizations. A course which has no practical job training and concentrates entirely on information about the company, its procedures and conditions of service, may require up to five days if each topic is dealt with in detail. It would be most unwise, however, to devote the whole of the first week at work to such a concentrated and indigestible menu. This type of course is best phased over a much longer period; perhaps one day a week for five weeks, or 10 half-days over a longer period.

The inclusion of practical job instruction in an initial training period enables the pure induction element to be similarly phased. For example, the induction element in the training programme for new recruits to a Fire Brigade is usually spread over the whole initial 12 weeks off the job training period. Highly active and practical job instruction on fire-fighting is interspersed with lecture-room sessions about the fire service, its history and traditions, and about more mundane matters such as conditions of service. The induction material is not all packed into the first week.

It is important to consider induction as a process which, though most obviously concerned with the first few days at work, extends over the much longer period between the employee starting work and eventually becoming fully integrated and competent. Induction courses should be seen as no more than the formalization of those elements of induction which are best met by systematic training. It follows that formal course attendance is best spread over a significant time period. The actual timing of each part of a course should be linked to an analysis of what information a new employee needs at various stages of the total induction process.

First day induction courses should therefore concentrate on the immediate practical issues needed to cope with life at work, while later modules can reflect and encourage the expanding interest of the new employee, first in the work of his or her immediate section or department, then to the wider setting of the company and the industry. This implies that some induction training sessions may best be scheduled for some months after the first day at work. For example, consider new professional staff (accountants, lawyers, engineers, etc) in a large multi-functional organization such as a company conglomerate or a large local authority. It is not immediately necessary for them to study the very wide or complex organizational setting in which the particular functions or subsidiary companies are located. Their first few months are likely to be fully occupied in adapting to their own specific work situations and departments. But after, say, three months, it may be timely to organize an induction module in which they can learn about, and discuss, the broader environment in which their immediate work functions are based.

General reference
This book does not attempt to describe the related subject of job training or the skills involved in instructing new employees in technical skills. For a detailed exposition of this topic, see:
Training in Industry and Commerce, SINGER E J, IPM, 1977 (new edition pending)

7
The induction course: techniques and content

It is inevitable that much induction training consists of imparting information, and rather less of developing specific working skills. Skills training may, of course, be a dominant feature in the first few weeks of employment for jobs in which recruits have little or no experience of the work concerned. The training of new firemen at Fire Brigade training centres has already been quoted as an example. Similar emphasis on job training occurs in many factories where new workers have to be trained, not in general skilled trades such as fitting, welding or bricklaying, but in machine operation or assembly techniques specific to the particular plant. Operator training of this kind lies outside the scope of this book, except to note that a good deal of induction training can be integrated with formal job training, and to suggest that some lessons can be learnt from skills training about the use of appropriate training techniques.

Induction training techniques

Much work has been done in developing different training techniques appropriate to various forms of job or skills training. Reliance on chalk and talk, or 'sitting by Nellie' has given way to a whole range of more relevant techniques, including discussion sessions, project work, and self-teaching methods through interactive computer systems. Less thought is often given to techniques for induction training, where 'giving a talk to the new starters' is often the only method used.

There are several good reasons for paying more attention to the techniques used in an induction course:

> nothing is more likely to result in a rapid loss of trainees' attention than a succession of talks. The following type of programme is a

recipe for boredom, frustration and a singular lack of success in securing an effective intake of information by the trainees:

9.30 am	Introductory talk by Factory Manager
9.15 am	History of the Company: talk by Personnel Manager
10.00 am	Conditions of employment: talk by Assistant Personnel Manager
10.45 am	Talk on sports and welfare: Company Welfare Officer
11.30 am	Safety in the factory: talk by Safety Officer etc

The use of a range of training methods creates the necessary variety to maintain the trainees' attention and involvement.

Different topics demand different training techniques. Films, slide-tape packages, video cassettes, wall-charts, overhead projector slides and other forms of visual aid will reinforce verbal forms of information and provide a more illustrative alternative to the straight talk. Any opportunity should also be taken of leaving the lecture room to see, rather than be told about, some aspect of the organization and its work. Why lecture about safety when a guided visit to the factory, plus some practical demonstrations, will make a far more vivid impact on the new recruits? Where the purpose of a session is to influence employees' attitudes (say, towards their role in a local authority *vis-à-vis* the general public), group discussions will be far more effective than lectures. Issues of this kind require new employees to think things through for themselves, albeit on a guided basis.

The lecture room is a very artificial environment, and listening to lectures is an activity very remote from the realities of working life. Training methods which take trainees out into the working environment, and which require their effort and involvement, are far more likely to serve the fundamental purpose of induction – easing the process of adaptation to actual work.

Checklist of techniques
A checklist of techniques other than talks illustrates the wide range of training methods to be considered when designing an induction course.

Films and video tapes: particularly to show aspects of an organization's work which are not readily accessible for new recruits to visit; and as a medium for communication by an otherwise remote top management in very large organizations. Films produced initially for publicity and job training purposes can often be used in an induction course.

Tape/slide packages: cheaper to produce than films (though not than video tapes if the training department has video equipment), and therefore more readily adaptable for specific induction purposes. Useful for explaining subjects which require a number of charts or diagrams. Can also (like films and videos) be produced centrally in a large organization and sent out for use by line managers.

Overhead projection transparencies: similar uses as slides, though supplementary to a conventional talk. Should be used to reinforce key points, and for fairly simple diagrams or charts. A typical example would be their use in a description of company organization structure.

Visits: guided visits to explain a factory operation or production sequence. These are an essential element in induction for which films are a second best, the latter only to be used if actual visits are wholly impracticable. A walk-through of any large building complex, pointing out the location of car parks, entrances, enquiry desks, canteen, rest and first aid rooms, etc, is also useful, though may need supplementing by a map.

Hand-outs: a variety of printed material should be used to supplement explanatory sessions, and provide a more permanent *aide-memoire* for the trainees. Employee handbooks can be talked through when explaining conditions of service and employment procedures. Some printed publicity material may reinforce films or visits. The company's annual report may provide useful explanatory and illustrative matter. Safety leaflets are also helpful.

Discussion groups: used much less generally for induction than in supervisory training, but a useful way of stimulating new recruits' interest in the organization's policies and objectives. For example, instead of merely telling new retail assistants of the firm's procedure for dealing with returned goods, a training session can start with the question: 'Why do you think we exchange returned goods without query?'

Projects and self-teaching methods: the discussion approach points towards discovery learning which represent methods in which new recruits have to find out information for themselves. Used particularly for 'A' level school-leavers and graduates, it may consist of giving a small group of new starters a couple of weeks to research a question such as 'What are the company's marketing strategies and how and why have these changed over the past five years?' Other groups may be given different aspects of the organization to study. All the groups are then brought together for a day, and each presents its findings to a group of senior managers who comment on, and if necessary correct, the information obtained. Other forms of self-teaching may include following a learning programme (eg use of a word processor) through a 'user-friendly' VDU terminal, with a training officer available to assist and check on progress.

Deciding the content

The actual subject matter of an induction course will be heavily influenced by such factors as:

(i) are the trainees new to the industry as well as to the particular organization? If so, then the course needs to include background information about the general economic or social setting.

(ii) are the trainees all destined for the same occupation? If so, induction training may be merged with normal job instruction. If not, the course will paint only a general picture of the working environment, leaving the detail either to a supplementary course specific to each job, or to normal on the job induction.

(iii) to what extent is useful induction material readily available (eg publicity films, job training packages, information packs) from national employers' organization or professional institutes? It is always worth researching the availability of suitable material from employers' associations, institutes, the Training Boards, government sources (Central Office of Information). What material, too, is available within the organization? Annual reports, employee handbooks, safety codes, advertising or publicity leaflets – all can be put to use in an induction course.

(iv) what is the volume of recruitment? Are induction courses required frequently or only occasionally? If frequently, they can be fairly comprehensive: if only occasionally, perhaps by grouping together once a quarter all the new starters for the past three months, much practical, initial induction will have to be left to line management.

(v) to what extent are line managers to be involved in the course? The danger of a course of any length run exclusively by personnel and training officers has already been referred to. If it is difficult for practical reasons to obtain line managers' involvement in the course (eg to talk about marketing policies; or to take part in a discussion about contacts with the public) then there is a case for restricting formal course content, and emphasizing systematic induction by line management within departments.

Checklist of content
The precise content of each course must therefore be tailored to fit the circumstances of the particular organization. As a checklist, however, the content is likely to need to include information about some or most of the following:

Domestic information
   geography of the site
   cloakrooms and lavatories
   canteen facilities
   rest and first aid rooms
   car parking, travelling arrangements
   time recording

Health and Safety
   fire exits and fire drills
   basic safety rules, no-smoking zones, etc
   accident procedures
   protective clothing
   occupational health service

Wages
   wage and salary systems
   bonus schemes, including employee shareholding, etc
   savings schemes
   allowances (shift, overtime, standby, etc)
   sick pay
   deductions

explanation of pay slip
actual pay-out procedure

Other conditions of service
hours of work, flexitime, rest breaks
annual leave, absence from work, extra-statutory holidays
pension scheme and life insurance
car and other expense claims
disciplinary procedures
grievance procedures
general rules and regulations

Welfare and other benefits
sports and social facilities
staff purchases
suggestion scheme
access to personal welfare counselling
mortgage assistance, loans

Trade unions and employee involvement
trade union membership requirements or policies
who's who: shop stewards, safety representatives
joint consultative systems, quality circles, briefing group system
pay bargaining systems; national and local agreements

Employee development
training schemes
assistance with professional studies, study leave, OU arrangements, etc
promotion opportunities and procedures
employee appraisal/review systems
qualification incentives

The organization itself
operational and other objective and policies
organization structure, role of constituent companies, departments, functions

    managerial and supervisory hierarchy and who's who
    scale: numbers employed, annual turnover, capital and revenue budget, etc
    processes, production methods, functions.
    public relations policies

The industry or sector

    nature and size of the industry or economic sector
    national/industrial organizations
    relationship with government
    relevant legislation affecting role, standards, functions, etc
    place of particular organization within whole industry or sector

Other items will need to be added to this list to meet the specific needs of particular categories of employees. Individual industries or sectors will also have their own unique characteristics which require explanation. Chapter 9 goes into this aspect in more detail.

8
Counselling and probation

The whole process of becoming acclimatized to a new job may take several months. Induction does not stop after the first day, nor should the planned element of induction be limited to attendance at an induction course.

There is a need to make regular checks on the progress of new employees (ie induction follow-up) and to take action to put right any aspect which is giving the employee or the employer cause for concern. The extent to which such follow-up is formalized varies. At one extreme, it may consist of no more than the occasional informal chat initiated by the supervisor. At the other extreme, it is a documented series of appraisal interviews with each new employee, with written reports being passed from supervisor to personnel officer, all set in the context of a formally specified probationary period.

Which method is right depends on the type of employee, the general employment ethos or style of the organization, the existence or otherwise of more general employee appraisal or counselling systems and to some extent, convention and tradition. Certainly, the formal probationary period is more common in the public than private sector, and this may reflect a generally greater emphasis on formality and documentation (not to say bureaucracy) in public sector organizations.

Whatever method of follow-up is used, the principle remains: that success in induction is enhanced by new employees' progress being closely monitored, and by any correcting assistance being provided to deal with any problems which may arise.

It is also important to ensure that induction and probation procedures conform to the requirements of employment legislation, particularly if dismissal for unsuitability or misconduct has to be considered. The first few months of employment are the only period during which the employer can take such action without the risk of being taken to an industrial tribunal. This should not be taken as an invitation to treat new employees less fairly than established staff. It does emphasize, however, the need to make a thorough assessment of each new employee's suitability, and to be consistent and systematic both in helping new employees to succeed and in terminating their employment if all reasonable efforts to achieve such success fail.

Progress checks

The period during which induction follow-up is advisable varies with the nature of the job. A fairly short period, say of less than three months, may be sufficient where the following factors apply:

> the work is simple, with no significant learning problems
>
> employees on this work form a major and stable occupational group within the organization
>
> the general pace and flow of work is steady, and not subject to frequent fluctuations of pressure or overtime
>
> existing employees have developed a welcoming and supportive attitude towards new recruits.

Much longer periods may be necessary in other circumstances, particularly where at least some of the following conditions exist:

> the work is complex and difficult to learn
>
> the work involves much subjective judgement, based on an acute understanding of, and 'feel' for, the internal attitudes or politics of the organization
>
> the job is outside the main, established routines of the organization
>
> there are large and unpredictable variations in workload, or sudden and significant overtime requirements interspersed with slack periods
>
> existing employees have developed an unusually closed or introverted culture which is perceived by newcomers to be unwelcoming or even hostile.

Lying behind the general principle of follow-up is the simpler view, often expressed by busy supervisors and hard-pressed personnel officers, that it is vital to weed out unsatisfactory employees at an early stage after recruitment. This is certainly a significant aspect of induction, though it should not set the tone for induction follow-up. New employees are unlikely to respond with enthusiasm to a management attitude which is dominated by thoughts of possible dismissal. To learn a new job quickly and well, and to adjust to the general mores of a new organization, the recruit requires support and assistance, not threats.

One element of follow-up is entirely informal: the day to day interest shown in the problems and progress of new employees by their supervisors and managers. Supervisory training courses should include a session about this, though the general approach is one which applies to the management of all employees, whatever their length of service. The new employee, however, will respond particularly well to the friendly but perceptive enquiry: 'Any problems, George? What about that installation procedure which was bugging you yesterday? Show me how its going now.' Note some subtleties about this apparently very informal enquiry:

> personal recognition; the use of a christian name. The employee is an individual being treated individually

> a reference to yesterday, showing that the supervisor remembers things of concern to the employee; another example of individual recognition

> a positive check on a specific aspect of the job, not just a very general enquiry which can too easily be answered by a possibly inaccurate: 'Alright, thanks'

> a request to the employee actually to demonstrate the particular work item involved, not merely to reply verbally.

The supervisor should also keep an eye open, too, for difficulties other than those related directly to the work. Symptoms of such difficulties may include late attendances, frequent short-term sickness absence, having to leave during the day because of the actual or alleged onset of such conditions as migraine or severe back-ache, fierce flashes of temper over very minor issues, a silent or withdrawn manner, or a marked failure to fit in with the social life of the working group. There can be a variety of reasons for these kinds of behaviour, and it is the supervisor's job to get to the bottom of any real problems and try to put things right. Typical underlying difficulties are:

> personality clashes with fellow employees, particularly those who are influential in the informal working group

disappointment with the job for a variety of reasons, such as it is proving less interesting, or generating lower earnings, than expected

worries about ability to cope, if not with the current work tasks then with what the employee perceives as future demands of the job

domestic problems, such as travel time proving longer than expected; or overtime requirements generating difficulties at home

personal dislike of the supervisor; a particularly difficult matter if the feeling is mutual.

This last point illustrates the value of a follow-up procedure which goes beyond the day to day actions of the supervisor. Progress or appraisal interviews with the personnel manager or the supervisor's manager after, say, one and three or six months service permit confidential discussion of such problems as dislike of the supervisor or domestic crises. Occasionally it may have to be faced that a serious personality mismatch has arisen between employee and supervisor, and that consideration may need to be given to a transfer, if this is practicable. From a range of these interviews from different departments, a personnel manager will also gain a useful insight into the differing abilities of individual supervisors in their staff management, and identify some who may need more training in relevant aspects of employee management.

If line managers conduct these follow-up interviews, they may do so to a pattern determined by a progress report form to be returned to the personnel department.

Checklist of progress reviews
There are a number of points about a new employee's progress which should be reviewed at regular intervals. These include:

Work output or productivity
Is the new employee progressing steadily from producing little or no output on the first day to the productivity levels expected of an experienced worker? Manual operations such as semi-skilled assembly work may be work-studied, with detailed output statistics produced for bonus and production planning purposes. In such circumstances it is possible to use output graphs for each new employee which compare progress with the average learning curve

for all workers. Fast or slow learners, or those hitting a bad patch in the learning process, can then be readily identified.

Some office work such as typing, word processing and computer in-putting can be similarly measured. In other jobs, a more subjective assessment may be needed.

Work quality
A fast rate of progress in terms of output is not always consistent with an absence of errors. What standard is the new employee reaching in qualitative terms? Does the rate of working need to be slowed down to improve quality? Is the new recruit taking so much trouble to avoid even the most minor of mistakes that output is suffering? As with output, quantified data about error rates are very useful when making such assessments, though with much administrative and professional work, statistical measurement is not possible.

Attitudes
What sort of attitude is the new employee displaying towards the job? Keen, interested and responsible? Worried, or apathetic or antagonistic? And if attitudes are negative, what are the apparent reasons? Is there any evidence of a serious mismatch between the employee's ability or aptitudes, and the demands and characteristics of the job?

Relationships
How is the new employee fitting into the work group? What is the quality of the supervisor/employee relationship? Are there any personality problems or problems of communication or compatibility? And as with all these questions, what corrective action might be taken (by the employee, the supervisor, or the personnel officer)?

Attendance
What is the employee's attendance record for sickness, other absences and lateness? If this is poor, are there any indications of the reasons.

Potential
Is the new employee showing any potential for more advanced or for different work, or for eventual supervisory or managerial work? It may be too early to consider transfers or promotion during the first few weeks or months of employment, but the indications of potential may well become evident at a very early stage and are worth noting

during these early progress reviews for later follow-up. (*See* chapter 9, page 60, for another comment on promotions and transfers).

An important result of such interviews should be positive action when this is required. The employee should know what is being done and why, and be told what standards or objectives are being set. For example, a decision may be made to transfer a not wholly satisfactory new employee from a very difficult factory assembly process to an easier type of work, with agreement between the supervisor and personnel manager that success on this easier work must be evident within four weeks or the employee's contract will be terminated. It is not unknown for such decisions to be effected with no clear explanation to the employee, who is thus unaware of failure on the difficult work or the risk of dismissal if this occurs on the work to which he is transferred. This is appallingly bad employment practice. The supervisor, perhaps with the personnel manager, should explain the decision and its reasons to the employee, set out what is now required in work performance, and encourage and assist the employee to make every effort to succeed. The four week deadline for a final decision about continued employment must be made crystal clear, preferably supported in writing (an absolute essential where formal probation is used which extends into the period when the employee has a right of access to an industrial tribunal for unfair dismissal).

The legal aspects of probation

The inclusion of a formal probationary period in a new employee's contract of employment has significant legal implications.

On the one hand, it may make it easier for the employer to dismiss an unsatisfactory recruit: on the other, there is an obligation on the employer properly to supervise an employee's progress during the probationary period.

A key case which helped to establish these principles was Post Office v Mughal[1]. The precise circumstances of this case are of less importance than the Employment Appeal Tribunal's statement about the questions to be answered when a probationer is dismissed:

> Has the employer shown that he took reasonable steps to maintain appraisal of the probationer during the period of probation, giving guidance by advice or warning when such is likely to be useful or fair: and that an appropriate officer made an honest effort to determine whether the probationer came up to the required

standard, having informed himself of the appraisals made by supervising officers and any other facts recorded about the probationer?

Note in this statement, the emphasis on *appraisal*, on *guidance* (advice or warning), and on the final decision as to whether or not the employee has reached a necessary standard being taken on the basis of the appraisal *reports*.

The EAT went on to say that if these steps are taken by the employer, then a dismissal will be fair provided only that the employer makes a reasonable decision about the probationer's suitability. Further, the EAT commented on six principles explained by the Post Office as governing their principles of probation:

1. Management must set the standards of capacity and efficiency required of a probationer if employment is to be confirmed. This inevitably involves management exercising an element of subjective judgement.
2. The employer takes on a probationer on trial and must decide whether the new recruit measures up to the standards set.
3. A probationer is, during a trial period, under continuous assessment and appraisal in a way that an ordinary employee is not.
4. As the probationer is on trial, and knows it, his failures may be strictly judged, as he should be reasonably regarded as trying to do his best.
5. In ordinary employment, it may not be easy for an employer to satisfy an industrial tribunal that he has fairly dismissed an employee who comes up to average in capacity and performance. But a probationer is liable to be dismissed if the employer can satisfy a tribunal that the probationer did not come up to the standard laid down for new recruits to the established (ie non-probationary) staff. If an ordinary employee has been below standard, but after warning improves, it is likely to be unfair to dismiss him for the inefficiency or misconduct which occurred before the warning. But in the case of a probationer, the employer is entitled to look at performance over the whole of the probationary period, and improved performance at the end of the period may not outweigh reasonable doubts about capacity or personality which are founded on the earlier period.

Said the EAT: 'We accept all those propositions'. In general, then, the EAT takes the view that although employers must make appraisals of probationers and take appropriate corrective action by way of advice or warnings, probationers themselves must accept that because they are on trial, their performance may reasonably be judged against higher standards than that of non-probationers.

There are numerous other dismissal cases on record which confirm these principles. In Cusack v London Borough of Camden[2] and Gray v Grenvil Associates[3] probationers' dismissals were held to be unfair because of inadequate supervision and counselling, and an absence of warnings.

In two other cases, O'Kelly v Royal Liver Friendly Society[4] and Schofield v Ray Alan Manshops[5], findings of unfair dismissals were influenced by a lack of training during the probationary periods.

These cases point to the value of telling the probationer to whom he should go with problems and on ensuring that this person, chargehand or supervisor, understands his responsibility of helping the newcomer to succeed.

The letter of appointment might usefully be quite specific on this point:

> During your probation X has been specifically assigned to look after you if you have any problems with your work. He/she is there to assist you and it is important that you take full advantage to ensure that you gain the greatest value from your probation period. If you are in doubt ask don't guess.

One other important point is clear from case law. That is, that employees who are treated by employers as 'on probation' must be told very clearly of this employment status. 'Probation' may be used loosely as a general phrase to describe an initial settling-in period. However, if the employer wishes to benefit from the ability to apply the strict standards set out in the Mughal case, it is essential that probationary status is clearly specified in the contract of employment[6].

How long should a probationary period be? Some employers have assumed that because a dismissed employee, working in an organization employing more than 20, has access to an industrial tribunal after 12 months service, a probationary period should not exceed 12 months. That is not the case and there is no obvious legal limit to the length of probation. It is nevertheless good employment practice for the probation period to be kept to a reasonable minimum. If probation is taken seriously (and there is no point in using probation unless this is so) it must be recognized as a period during which new employees have a very serious uncertainty hanging over them. Will their employment be confirmed? It would be poor personnel management to maintain this period of uncertainty longer than absolutely necessary. The actual period, then, has to be related to the nature of the job, and to a realistic assessment of the time taken for an acceptable recruit to reach an acceptable standard.

In some simple jobs this might be as short as a month: in more complex work, six months to a year are not unusual or unreasonable.

Regardless of the precise length of probation, or indeed of whether a formal probationary period exists at all, it is essential that all new employees are assessed for suitability after 10 to 11 months' service. This is the last opportunity to terminate employment before the risk of a tribunal action for unfair dismissal. A failure to consider long term suitability at this critical point can lead to serious difficulties if the unsatisfactory employee is allowed to continue after the first 12 months.

Access to an industrial tribunal begins after one year's service (two years if the organization has less than 20 employees). In considering dismissals of new employees it must be noted that if a notice period extends beyond this 12 months point, then the right of tribunal access is obtained, even though notice was given before the 12 months expired. It is the date of the last day in employment which establishes the length of service, not the date on which a dismissal notice was issued. The only way of avoiding this trap, should a decision about dismissal be delayed until very close to the 12 month point, is to dismiss summarily (ie without notice) and pay money in lieu of notice. It is essential that any dismissal letter is explicit about the date of the last day in employment.

Probation documents

Three forms of documentation are needed to ensure that all the requirements of probation are met:

1. A statement in the letter of appointment or in the terms and conditions of employment, specifying the probationary status and its duration.
2. At the very least, one document (report or managerial memo) which provides evidence of an assessment of suitability for permanent employment. If the outcome of probation is dismissal, documented evidence of appraisals and of attempts at corrective action such as advice, training and warnings is highly desirable.
3. Written notification to the employee stating the outcome of this

assessment. This might be confirmation of the satisfactory completion of probation, dismissal, or extension of probation.

A typical statement in the letter of appointment would be:

> This appointment is initially on a probationary basis for a period of six months, though this period may be extended if it is decided that more time is needed to assess your suitability for normal/ permanent/established employment.

> (*The exact phraseology for non-probationary employment varies. Public sector organizations often distinguish between probationary and 'established' status*).

The wording must indicate that employment will continue beyond the probationary period if all goes well. Without any such reference (direct or implied) the employee might argue that the job is for a fixed term contract, thus acquiring security of employment for the whole of the probationary period[7]. The appointment letter should therefore also indicate that employment may be terminated during, as well as at the end of, the probationary period. For example: 'Your employment may be terminated at any time during the probationary period if you are considered for any reason to be unsuitable for continued employment.'

The form of documented assessment depends on the appraisal and reporting systems in use. It may consist of the completion by the supervisor or manager of a standard appraisal form, designed and issued by the personnel department. It may be a standard report, completed by the personnel manager after discussions with the employee and the supervisor. It may be a less structured document, such as a memo from the supervisor to the personnel department; though in any large organization a standard format is desirable to ensure consistency of approach across all departments. It may also be part of the letter to the employee, giving formal notification of the outcome of probation.

This latter approach is acceptable where probation has been completed satisfactorily. A letter may then say:

> I am pleased to tell you that you have completed your probationary period satisfactorily, and I can therefore confirm your continued employment on a normal/established/permanent basis from . *date* . .

Extending a probationary period

A common practice of notifying probationers of the outcome of probation only if a dismissal or extension of probation is decided is to be deprecated. The employee who is told nothing at the end of probation may well be uncertain as to whether this indicates the beginning of normal employment, or dissatisfaction with his or her performance. In one case on record (Walker v Woolley)[8] it was held that the absence of confirmation should have been treated by the employee as a form of warning. It seems highly desirable to avoid misunderstanding and worry, by a positive statement in all circumstances.

If progress has not been entirely satisfactory, the letter will need to make more specific reference to the results of assessment. Thus, for example:

> Your initial period of probationary service is due to end on *date*.
>
> You will know from our recent discussion, however, that I am not yet wholly satisfied about your suitability for continued normal employment. In particular, I need to see a sustained improvement in the following aspects of your work:

(*give details of shortcomings and reminders of advice and warnings*).

> I have therefore decided that the period of probationary service should be extended until *date*. If you maintain a satisfactory standard during this period, your continued employment will then be confirmed, and I hope very much that this will be the outcome. If, however, you fail to achieve and maintain the required standards I must now place on record that your employment will be terminated.

A follow-up discussion at this stage is also essential if employer and employee are going to work together to secure success.

For how long might a probationary period continue to be extended? There are no absolute rules about this: it is a matter of reasonableness and common sense. It is obviously undesirable to put off almost indefinitely the important decision as to whether or not a new employee is suitable. It is also questionable practice unilaterally to extend a probationary period if no mention of extensions has been made in the formal conditions of employment. As a very rough rule of thumb, one extension of between a quarter and half the length of the initial period seems a reasonable limit in other than very unusual cases.

Extending a probationary period beyond 12 months will not, of course, evade the 12 month trap of the employee's right of access to an industrial tribunal. That right will accrue regardless of the status of employment. If, however, the probationary period has been unambiguously extended for clearly explained reasons, as in the example given above, an eventual dismissal for failure to improve within the terms of the letter extending probation is almost certain to be supported at a tribunal, provided that clear evidence is given of the employee's shortcomings and of reasonable efforts by the employer to correct them.

References

1 EAT 243/76 and IRLR 5th May, 1977
2 COIT 917/195, 1979
3 COIT 831/171, 1978
4 COIT 882/212, 1979
5 COIT 818/90, 1978
6 For a summary of case law regarding probation *see* 'Capability Dismissals', IDS Brief, Supplement no 28, June, 1980.
7 Dalgleish v Kew House Farms (1982) IRLR 251
8 COIT 337/210, 1975
9 For a description of appraisal interviewing applicable to progress reviews, see *Effective Performance Review Interviews*, Robinson K, IPM, 1983

9
Needs of particular groups

Most of the previous chapters have dealt with induction principles and procedures which are common to all new employees, from school leavers taking up basic manual or clerical work to newly recruited managers. It has been stressed, however, that the design of particular induction schemes should take into account the specific characteristics of different types of work. This chapter examines some of the different induction needs of some particular occupational groups.

School leavers

School leavers have one unique characteristic: their lack of experience of paid employment. With adult recruits, even those starting jobs different from anything they have previously undertaken, the employer can assume their general experience of the disciplines of employment. But the employer who offers a school leaver his or her first job should recognize a responsibility to assist the youngster make a successful entry to the world of work, as well as coping with the particular job.

Induction for school leavers consequently merits more thorough attention than for any other group. Four broad areas of learning and adaptation are involved:

> adjustment to working in a defined job role, in a structured environment, within prescribed rules and procedures

> understanding the general industrial, commercial or other setting in which the employing organization is based

> understanding the nature and functions of the employing organization itself

> learning the actual job.

Although it is the last which is the most obvious, and to the busy supervisor the most urgent, success in learning the job is enhanced by attention being paid to the other three factors.

Perhaps the most thorough definition of the training needs of school leavers has been set out by the Manpower Services Commission for the Youth Training Scheme (YTS)[1]. A YTS programme, applicable equally to normally recruited youngsters as to those on temporary scheme placements, should include the following features within a 12 month training period.

Direct induction: a planned, systematic introduction to the particular scheme and to the workplace, spread over a period (not limited to the first day or week) and linked with the other training elements in the scheme.

Initial assessment: an early assessment of the trainee's needs, preferences and capabilities.

Planned work experience: properly supervised job experience, planned to achieve defined learning objectives.

Core skills: training in skills common to almost all jobs; communication skills, problem solving methods, job-oriented numeracy, computer literacy and the like.

Occupationally oriented training: training in the skills common to a general occupational group. This requires not just the narrow training necessary to cope with one particular job, but a range of training relevant to the general category of work. For clerical trainees, for example, training should include such matters as use of telephones, principles of classification and filing, business letter writing, use of office equipment (eg photocopiers, dictation systems, etc).

Off the job training: a minimum of three months of all the various elements of training to be conducted off the job. Courses may be provided in local colleges, or on employers' premises (ie company training centres). Training course attendance may be in any suitable form (block or day release, or modules of various duration) spread throughout the 12 months.

Reviews and records: trainees' progress to be reviewed at regular intervals and the results documented.

Counselling: a properly trained, nominated senior person (eg personnel or training officer) to liaise with line supervisors, and if necessary with colleges and the local education authority's careers service, to ensure guidance and counselling throughout the scheme.

In the MSC's view, this pattern of training should be adopted for the first 12 months of every school-leaver's employment. It forms a most useful and comprehensive set of guidelines against which each organization can design its own tailor-made scheme for the proper induction and job training of its school leaver recruits.

Graduates

The graduate entrant with no previous working experience has very similar induction needs to the school leaver. Graduates do not require quite such a basic approach: they are older, and their university experience should have gone some way to developing their self-confidence and self-teaching abilities. Many, of course, will also have had vacation employment, often in usefully humble jobs which will have opened their eyes to the reality of life on the factory or office floor.

Partly because of the jobs they are aiming for on a career basis, partly because of their academic experience generating (hopefully) an intellectually enquiring approach, their induction needs to pay more attention than with school leavers to a study of the industrial and organizational setting in which their particular initial jobs are based. For example, a graduate joining a food processing company will want to know about the food industry generally (its scale, market and technical trends, export experience, etc.) the role of the particular company within the industry, and the company's own sales, development, production, financial and organizational policies and objectives. A graduate entrant to a local government administrative post in, for example, a social services department, will need to understand the nature of local government as a statutorily defined decision-making institution, how it obtains its resources, how it allocates resources between its various functions, and what the particular role of its social services department is within the total framework of a local authority.

Normal induction activities (short courses, planned work experience, visits) can all be used. One other method, particularly suited to graduates, can exploit their academically developed ability to learn for themselves. This is to give graduates, either individually or in small groups, some form of investigatory project which necessitates them finding out for themselves much of the facts about their organization and its setting.

For example, a group of four or five graduate trainees in a large local authority might be given details of a small town which is suffering from traffic congestion. They would be asked to report back to a panel of managers on the steps which would be necessary to assess the pros and cons of alternative routes for a bypass. They would be expected to discover that a very wide range of council functions would be involved (engineering, legal, financial, environmental, political) while the task of presenting a complex issue by written report and verbal explanation is also excellent and relevant job training. In an industrial setting, projects might include such issues as the possible closure of a factory, the launching of an export drive, or the impact of robotics.

Ethnic minorities

Recruits from ethnic minorities will be particularly sensitive to the personal and group attitudes of their fellow workers and supervisors, and to the general social culture of the workplace. Personnel managers and supervisors should be alert to problems which could arise, quite unintentionally, from the peculiarities of the organization's formal and informal traditions and styles.

Particular attention needs to be paid, too, to any latent or actual friction between individuals. Some discussion may well be necessary between supervisor and existing employees should actual or apparent racially biased attitudes prejudice successful induction.

Apart from this general factor, language training can be one specific requirement in some circumstances. This is particularly needed where Asian women are recruited, though for other groups, too, training in the specific jargon and language of the trade is often desirable. Where large numbers of ethnic minority recruits are involved, it may also be helpful to have recruitment and induction literature available in their own languages (eg Urdu) as well as in English.

Industrial or occupational groups

Each industry, or other form of organization or institution, has its own unique characteristics, problems or hazards which need to be explained to new recruits. It is not practicable to provide a comprehensive list, but examples are:

(i)   Agriculture – handling of toxic chemicals used in crop and pest control – safe tractor driving methods.
(ii) Banking – confidentiality of customer information – security systems.
(iii) Catering and food industries – personal and working hygiene.
(iv) Construction – hazards and safety rules for each site – procedures regarding disposal of scrap.
(v)   Health service – procedures and style of patient contacts – inter-functional relationship of administrative, nursing and medical staff.
(vi) Hotels – dealing with guests – guests' lost property procedures.
(vii) Local government – relations between officers and elected members – conduct regarding hospitality by suppliers.
(viii) Manufacturing industry – hazards specific to each trade eg woodworking machinery in furniture trade: handling of radio-active isotopes: no-smoking zones, etc – product security regulations (ie searches of employee cars, bags, etc)
(ix) Retailing – customer complaints procedures – staff purchasing regulations.
(x)   Gas, electricity, water – for outside staff, rules about production of identity cards to the public – for sales and service staff, customer relations and customer complaints procedures.

Personnel managers should, of course, produce their own comprehensive schedules of such key points specific to their particular sectors and organizations.

Managers

Because managers are usually recruited individually, and because their role often makes it difficult or inappropriate for them to be merged with more junior staff in a formal induction programme, their induction needs are often wholly overlooked.

Yet the effectiveness of new managers can be achieved more quickly if at least some elements of their first few weeks are systematically planned. The main needs are usually:

- to get to know the formal and informal hierarchy and power structure of the organization

- to meet not only their immediate seniors and juniors, but also all the other managers in other departments with whom their jobs involve contact

- to know the formal limits of their authority to make decisions without reference to higher or other levels

- to understand the informal expectations of other managers (and the trade unions) to be consulted before decisions are made, even when the formal rules appear to permit unilateral decision making

- to discover the best sources of information and advice, inside and outside the organization

- to understand the nature and emphases in the organization's external relations.

It is consequently very helpful for the manager to be given a carefully prepared reading package of relevant reports, key company memoranda, organization charts, policy and procedure documents, the most important of the correspondence files, minutes of management meetings, and perhaps an annotated list of the main personalities with whom the job involves contact.

Cold print alone is not enough, and a programme of visits and discussions with relevant managers should be arranged for the first week or so. The personnel manager and the manager's own senior need to talk through and explain this programme with the new manager. The personnel manager has a particular role in these introductory discussions:

- to describe the *informal* style, methods, and groupings in the organization, particularly where these differ from the formal structure and procedures

- to explain the key elements of the organization's personnel policies and procedures as they impinge on the day to day work of the line manager.

During the manager's induction period, it may also be helpful to arrange for him or her to sit in on various management meetings and on relevant joint consultative meetings with the trade unions, mainly to observe the organization in action and to be introduced to colleagues and working contacts.

The new manager's senior should be particularly aware of the difficulty any newcomer has of adapting rapidly to the style and standards of an organization, with the consequent risk that some of the manager's first decisions may be logically sound, but tactically unsatisfactory. Tactful initial assistance with more sensitive issues can help to avoid the risk of the morale-shattering *faux-pas*.

Transfers and promotions

If there is one group of employees whose induction needs are overlooked even more frequently than managers, it is an organization's own staff who move to new jobs on transfer or promotion.

The degree of change involved in such a job change does, of course, vary considerably. At one extreme is the clerk who merely takes over a similar job in the same office. Here, there is no real need for induction, only for a systematic explanation of the requirements of the new job. But at the other extreme is the technician in a factory in Doncaster, promoted to a head office technical sales job in London. In this case, only the name of the employer and a few conditions of service such as the pension scheme remain unchanged. Otherwise, the degree of change is very much greater than for a completely new employee, already a London-based technical sales representative in the same industry, who joins the same sales office as the promotee. The new recruit already knows the industry, the type of job and the location. The promotee has to make all these adjustments at once, while also coping with the domestic upheaval of moving home.

Personal counselling by the London personnel manager, and on the job coaching by the technical sales manager, can do much to ease this difficult transition.

Organizations with a sufficient inflow of new recruits to run formal induction courses on a regular basis would do well to consider transferred and promoted employees for attendance for at least parts of the courses. Existing employees will not take kindly to being treated as completely raw recruits. They will wish to be recognized as having already acquired valuable knowledge and experience of, for example, the industrial processes, the company organization structure, and many of the employment rules and conditions. Selective attendance at those sessions of an induction course which cover new ground is therefore needed, and it is a sound approach for the personnel manager to discuss the course programme with transferees and agree with them which sessions will be useful.

Practical circumstances may make it difficult for them to flit in and out of particular sessions. The course may, for example, be held at a different location from their work base so that whole day attendances or nothing are the only choice. In these cases, the transferees' or promotees' knowledge of the organization can be turned to good effect by arranging for them to assist the course organizers in running those sessions on which their attendance would otherwise be unnecessary.

There is a much wider aspect to promotions and transfers than the induction element. Decisions to transfer or promote should be seen by both the employee and the organization as logical steps in a whole process of career development. What is needed to achieve this is a systematic staff development policy in which periodic assessments of performance and potential occur throughout an employee's working life, not merely during the few months after starting a new job[2]. It is far easier to design an effective induction element within this wider process, than to introduce systematic internal induction as a single procedure unrelated to any general pattern of staff development.

References

1 *Setting up and running Youth Training Programmes*, SINGER E J and JOHNSON R, IPM, 1983
2 For a description of a wider approach to staff development, see *Manpower Training and Development*, KENNEY J, DONELLY E and REID M, IPM, 1979

10
The role of the personnel department

This book has described a wide range of induction activities which involve personnel officers, line managers and supervisors. In job training, and in helping the new employee adjust to life at the workplace, managers and supervisors play a most important role. Personnel managers cannot achieve effective induction by themselves: it requires a joint approach by the personnel and line departments.

It is nevertheless useful to identify the specific role of the personnel manager and four main elements of induction work which should be undertaken by the personnel department:

(i) the design of induction policies and procedures
(ii) the implementation of particular aspects of the induction process
(iii) monitoring the operation of the organization's induction practices
(iv) providing a welfare and counselling service to new employees to help them overcome induction problems.

Designing policies and procedures

The evolution of an effective induction policy is very much part of the personnel manager's general responsibility for developing effective employment practices. This policy should embrace the whole range of induction activities, from pre-employment procedures, through initial induction training to later follow-up and to the decision about new employees' suitability which needs to be made by the eleventh month of employment.

The objectives of an induction policy are to assist new employees to adapt rapidly to their jobs, to help them become effective in their work as quickly as possible in order to reduce initial learning costs, and to create an enthusiastic, co-operative and adaptable workforce.

Ultimately, as with all personnel policies, the objective is maximum organizational efficiency so that the company can improve its business competitiveness, or (as in the public sector) so that the organization can provide the most efficient and cost-effective service possible.

Implementing an induction policy requires the co-operation of all managers and supervisors, and will involve some commitment of time and resources, particularly into various forms of training. An induction policy, while initiated by the personnel manager, therefore needs to be discussed with and agreed by top management. Any initial reluctance to take induction seriously can be countered by the personnel manager demonstrating the costs and other adverse effects of a high level of early leaving, or of low morale, slow learning and poor performance among new starters.

An important aspect of induction policy is to ensure a consistent approach throughout all the stages of induction, and to obtain compatibility between the style and function of the organization and the impressions and information which the induction process generates in the new employee.

Consistency means that if selection and recruitment procedures are highly structured, then later stages of induction should be similarly structured. Sudden changes of style or pace between different stages of induction can be most disconcerting and do not achieve the steady progression from apprehensive raw recruit to confident experienced worker which well-planned induction can produce.

The need for compatibility between the general style of the induction process and the character of the organization has been mentioned in earlier chapters. It bears re-emphasis here. There is no point in the personnel manager designing a highly formalized set of induction procedures if the whole style of the organization is one of relaxed informality. That type of organization requires a relaxed, systematic but informal induction process.

Examples of induction policies

An induction policy needs first to consider these very general points about the character or style of the procedures which will best fit the nature of the organization. More specifically, it should specify the key elements or requirements of the system. It might specify, for example:

(i) That within the selection process, all short-listed candidates

(ii) will be interviewed by their potential section supervisor and be given a short tour of their prospective work-place.

(ii) That all selected applicants will be issued with a copy of the company handbook and of relevant sales or information literature about the organization with the formal offer of employment.

(iii) That all departments will produce a checklist of induction action to be taken on the first and subsequent days of work; with responsibility for various aspects of induction allocated to named members of staff.

(iv) That all managers, supervisors and other staff involved in the induction process will attend relevant training courses.

(v) That all new employees will attend a three day off the job induction course within their first three months of employment.

(vi) That the progress of each new employee will be reviewed and reported after one, three and 10 months.

(vii) That a positive decision to continue or discontinue employment will be made for every new employee in time for dismissal to be effected before the completion of 12 months service.

This is not an exhaustive list: it illustrates the type of induction action which it is helpful to specify in an induction policy in order to obtain systematic and consistent treatment of new employees, and to secure line management commitment and involvement.

Personnel department's own tasks

The precise allocation of responsibility for different parts of the whole induction process to the personnel department or to line management will obviously vary. Organizations with a large number of small subsidiary establishments (shops, area offices, small factories) are likely to depend more on line managers than large, centralized organizations in which the personnel department may handle most of induction except for on the job training.

It is unusual, however, for the personnel department not to be directly responsible for most, if not all, the following functions:

(i) Designing and drafting most of the pre-employment documents, ie application forms, contract of employment documents, employee handbooks, information leaflets, standard letters giving first day instructions and the like.

(ii) Conducting selection interviews and notifying applicants of the results.
(iii) Informing line managers of the starting dates of new employees.
(iv) Meeting new starters, dealing with first day documentation, and providing starters with at least some of their initial induction information.
(v) Planning and administering formal induction courses.
(vi) Within these courses, running sessions which explain the conditions of service, company rules, welfare and social facilities, career development schemes and other employment matters.
(vii) Planning and co-ordinating progress checks on new employees and often conducting follow-up or counselling interviews with new starters.
(viii) Planning and running training sessions on various aspects of induction to ensure that line managers, supervisors, and job trainers can perform their induction tasks effectively.
(ix) Advising line managers on action to deal with unsatisfactory new employees and, if necessary, administering the dismissal procedure.

Monitoring

It is one thing to have a set of defined induction policies and procedures. It is another to ensure that they are effectively operated, or that in operation they achieve the desired results. The personnel department should take an over-view of the whole induction process in order to monitor its effectiveness and if necessary to modify or develop the process.

Statistics

Early leaving is the major symptom of poor induction. The recording and analysis of labour turnover among new employees is therefore a most important part of the monitoring role. Statistically, this has several dimensions:

(i) The volume of early leaving (eg employees with under one year's service) as a proportion of all leavers. This analysis will show the extent to which total labour turnover of all employees consists of early leavers.
(ii) The numbers and percentages of each month's or year's newly

(iii) An analysis of the length of service of all leavers which is perhaps the most useful statistic of all. At monthly or quarterly intervals this analysis might show the numbers and percentages of leavers with service of:
recruited employees who are still in employment at specified later dates. This form of stability analysis will show the incidence of turnover at different lengths of service.

Less than one week
One to 12 weeks
13–26 weeks
27–52 weeks
1–5 years
5–10 years
10–20 years
Over 20 years.

As with all statistics, these figures are of maximum value when kept consistently over a long time period. A study of trends is often of more value than any one set of figures at a particular date.

To obtain the most value from statistics of the type just described, it may be helpful to produce them in two forms:

(i) by occupational category
(ii) by department or section.

Analyses of occupational categories, craft, non-craft manual, general clerical, sales, technical, etc will reveal significant differences which may highlight the need for improved induction for a whole occupational group across all departments.

Analyses of the early leaving patterns of each department may reveal significant differences for the same occupational group between different workplaces. One department, for example, may be achieving much more stability among its non-craft manuals than other similar departments. What is being done differently here? The answers may well result in improved induction across the whole organization.

Other aspects
Not all monitoring can be effected through statistics. Some aspects will require the more direct involvement of the personnel manager. These are likely to include:

(i) Interviewing early leavers to probe the real reasons for such resignations. As well as solving individual problems, the personnel manager should look for patterns and trends. Is one particular supervisor perceived by new employees as unhelpful or antagonistic? Is there widespread disillusionment about earnings or job interest? Are some particular elements of one type of work generating serious learning or training problems?

(ii) Checking that departments are using their induction checklists and are nominating the right employees for training in induction techniques. Do job trainers understand the learning problems of new recruits? Are new employees being shown the right things on their first day? Does the supervisor take progress checking seriously?

(iii) Reviewing the impact made on new employees of off the job induction training. Do the new starters understand the material used in these courses? Do the courses cover the points which may be worrying new employees? Do supervisors report any improvement in new starters' interest or understanding after attendance at these courses?

(iv) Studying the progress reports made by supervisors on new employees for problems and trends.

Welfare and counselling

It is particularly helpful to new employees to know that there is somewhere and someone they can go to with their worries or problems; and that they will there receive a sympathetic and confidential hearing. This is not a matter of the personnel manager usurping the employee management role of the departmental head or section supervisor. Some of the points raised by new employees may well need to be put back into the line manager's court. The personnel manager must also encourage new starters to lose their sense of newness as quickly as possible and to stand on their own feet in their own sections. The new employee who runs to the personnel department with the slightest problem needs kindly but firmly to be redirected back to the supervisor on all those points best dealt with at the workplace.

But there is a need for continuity of contact with a known person throughout the various stages of getting a new job and becoming acclimatized to a new organization. The personnel officer who is met at the selection interview is the best placed to become this helpful and familiar face during the first few difficult weeks or months.

Furthermore, the new starter should be positively encouraged to seek an interview with the personnel officer if worries develop about things which the new starter may think it difficult to discuss with the supervisor. The supervisor may, of course, be the very problem which the new employee wants to talk about. Short service employees who become discouraged and resign often do so over issues which, if discussed confidentially with the personnel officer, might well have been resolved.

Handling this confidential role is not an easy one. It requires a nice balance to be struck between regard for the new employee, the needs of the organization, and the role and sensitivities of line managers and supervisors. The personnel manager must always bear in mind that the ultimate objective is the effectiveness and efficiency of the organization, not the solving of welfare problems *per se*. But, of course, the exercise of judgement of this kind is the essence of much of the work of a personnel manager throughout the whole personnel function, of which induction forms only one (though an important) part.

Index

advertisements, job 13, 14
agreements, national 16
agriculture 58
annual company reports 16
appointment, letters of 14, 50
appraisal and counselling 7, 40, 42, 51, 56, 60, 62, 67, 68
aptitude tests 9
attendance records 44, 46
attitudes to work 10, 44, 46

banking 58
bonus schemes 8, 39
boredom 8, 36, 45

career prospects 1, 8, 40, 60, 61
catering and canteens 18, 22, 25, 39, 58
clerical workers 4, 9
cloakrooms and lavatories 23, 25, 39
closed shop agreements *see* **trade unions**
clothing 18
conditions of employment 8, 40
construction industry 58
contract of employment 16, 17, 47, 49
costs *see* **recruitment**
counselling *see* **appraisal**

development, employee *see* **career prospects**
disciplinary procedures 40
discovery learning 37, 38
discrimination 14
discussion groups 30, 36, 37
disillusionment 5, 8, 13, 33
dismissal 6, 9, 44, 47, 48, 49

documents, employment 16, 18, 21, 27, 64
documents, probation 50–53
domestic problems 45
draughtsmen 5

early leaving 3–11, 63, 65
earnings and wage systems 8, 13, 39, 45
Employment Appeal Tribunal 47, 48
employment, full 3
equal opportunities 14, 57
equipment manuals 27
extension of probation 50–53
ethnic minorities 57

factory work *see* **manufacturing**
films 30, 31, 32, 36, 38
firemen 4, 33
first day at work 9, 15, 17, 20–29, 31, 65
follow-up *see* **progress checks**
foremen *see* **supervisors**

graduates 38, 56–57
group psychology, attitudes, etc 10, 11, 31, 43, 46, 57

handbooks, employee 16, 23, 37, 38, 64
health service 58
hotels 58

identity cards and security 18, 22
induction courses 30–41, 64, 65, 67
induction policies 62–64
induction, pre-employment 13–19

69

industry, background information about   41
interviews, appraisal   42
interviews, exit   11, 66, 67
interviews, selection   14, 15, 65

Japanese management practice   24
job descriptions   17, 27, 28
job instruction   *see* **training, job**

labour stability   4, 66
labour turnover   1, 3, 4, 13, 65
language training   57
lectures   35, 36
legal aspects   17, 42, 47–50
legislation, employment   *see* **legal aspects**
literature, company and sales   16, 27
local government   24, 33, 58

managers' induction   16, 20, 32, 58–60
managers, role of   9, 14, 20, 39
manual workers   3, 4
manufacturing industry and factory work   3, 24, 31, 35, 58
medical examinations   18

occupational health   39
offices and office work   9, 17, 24, 27, 28
organizations, style and structure   10, 37, 40
output and productivity   5, 45
overtime   5, 8, 16, 43

parking arrangements   18, 22, 25, 39
pension schemes   16
personality clashes   9, 44, 45
personnel manager, role of   6, 11, 30, 62–68
police   4
Post Office v Mughal   47
probation   42, 47–53
procedures, job systems and schedules   9, 28
professional staff   4, 33

progress checks   42, 43–47, 64
projects   37, 38
promotion and potential   40, 46, 60, 61
public utilities   58

quality of work   46

reception arrangements   20, 21
recruitment costs   5
recruitment procedures   8, 9, 13, 38
resignations   1, 3, 8, 10, 11
retailing   24, 31, 58

safety and first aid   22, 24, 36, 39
sales jobs   13
school leavers   16, 20, 38, 54
selection procedures   9, 15, 63
self-teaching   27, 38
shop stewards   29
starter's friend   25
starting instructions   17, 18
statistics   65–66
supervisors, role of   9, 14, 15, 23, 26
supervisors, training of   24, 44, 64, 65

tape-slide packages   37
techniques of training   30, 31, 35–41
timekeeping   17, 21, 22, 23, 24, 39, 44
trade union functions and membership   22, 29, 40, 59
training, job   5, 26, 33, 38, 55
transfers   27, 46, 47, 60, 61
tribunals, industrial   6, 42, 47, 50
tutor, job   26

unemployment   3, 6

videos   36
visits to workplace   15, 31, 36, 37, 58

wages   *see* **earnings**
welfare   6, 40, 62, 67, 68
working groups   *see* **group psychology**

Youth Training Scheme   55–56